MY FIRST
THEORY BOOK

Lina Ng

© RHYTHM MP SDN. BHD. 1985
Revised Edition 1995
New Edition: 2001

Sole Distributor:
RHYTHM MP SDN. BHD.
2060 & 2061, Jalan Persekutuan, Permatang Tinggi Light Industry,
14000 Seberang Perai Tengah, Penang, Malaysia.
Tel: 04-5873689 (Direct Line), 04-5873690 (Hunting Line)
Fax: 04-5873691
E-mail: rhythm_mp@mphsb.po.my

Published by
RHYTHM MP SDN. BHD.

Cover Design by
LIM WAI FUN

Pre-press by
CP TECH SDN. BHD.

Printed in Malaysia by
MONOSETIA SDN. BHD.

ISBN 967-985-441-8
Order No.: MPM-3002-01

Rhythm MP

CONTENTS  My

TREBLE & BASS

Treble Clef / G Clef (**Cuts the G-line**)

Bass Clef / F Clef (**Starts on F**)

homework!

NUMBER OF COUNTS

Semibreve

| 4 | 4 | 4 | 4 | 4 | 4 | 4 |

Dotted Minim

| 3 | 3 | 3 | 3 | 3 | 3 | 3 |

Minim

| 2 | 2 | 2 | 2 | 2 | 2 | 2 |

Crotchet

| 1 | 1 | 1 | 1 | 1 | 1 | 1 |

Write the number of counts.

| 4 | 3 | 2 | 1 | 3 | 4 | 1 | 2 |

| 2 | 4 | 1 | 4 | 3 | 1 | 2 | 3 |

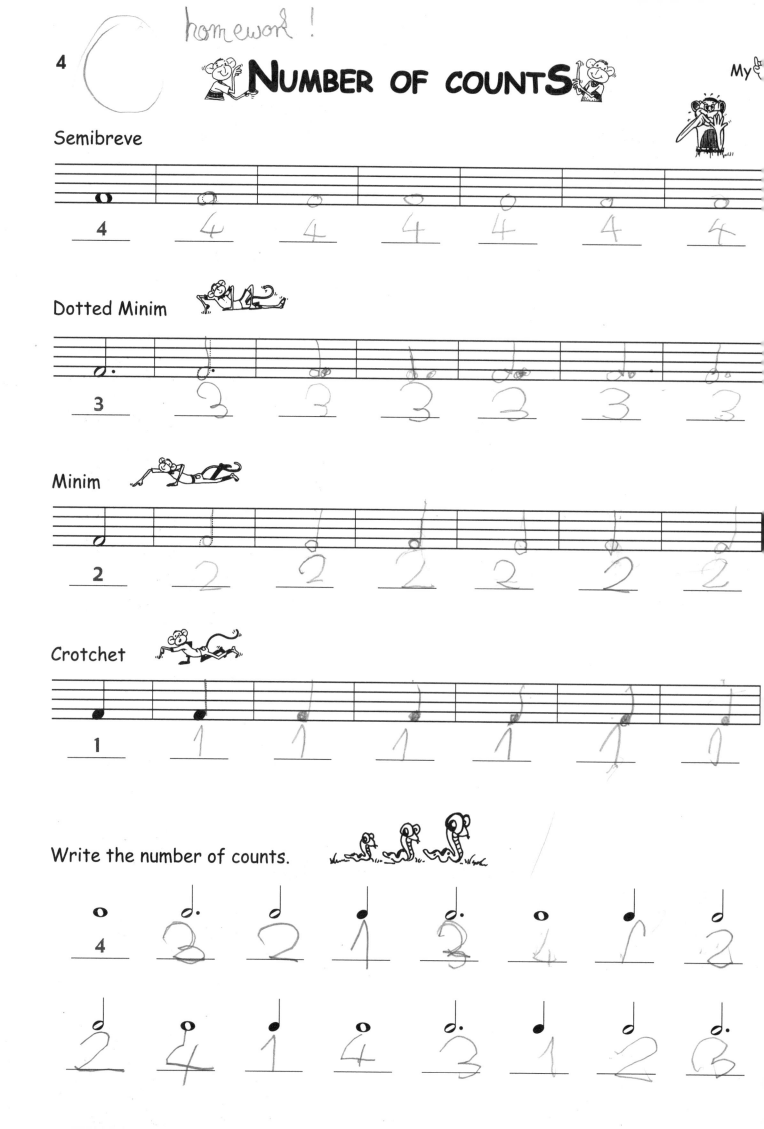

BALLOONS FOR SALE

Colour the balloons accordingly.

NO. OF COUNTS	COLOUR
1	RED
2	BLUE
3	YELLOW
4	GREEN

rouge
bleue
jaune
vert

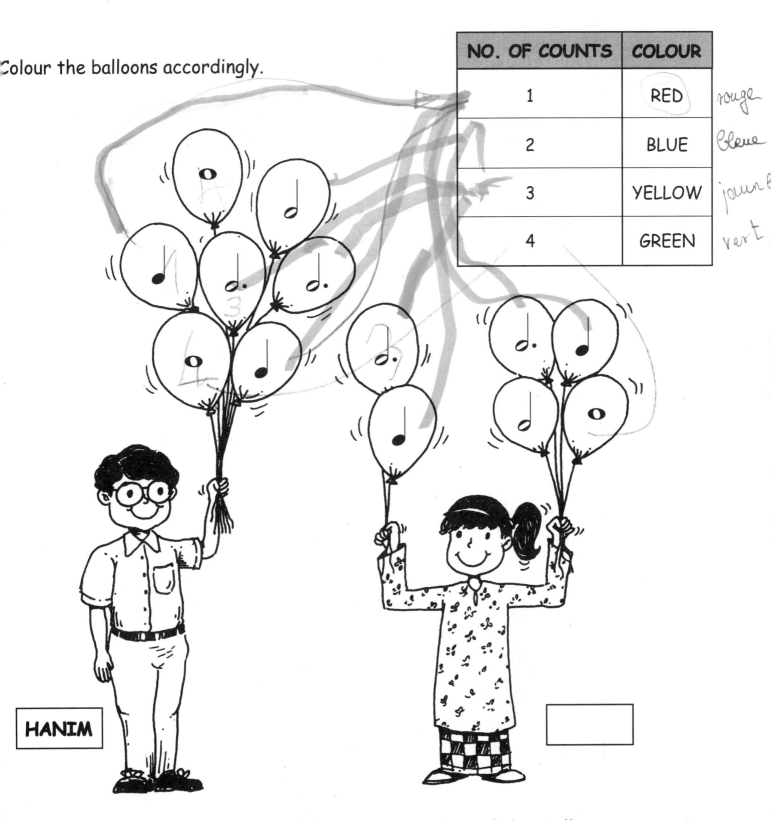

HANIM

Oh-oh, Hanim has one extra balloon. What is the colour of that balloon?

___ ___ ___ ___ ___

Spell Hanim's name from right to left to find out his sister's name.

___ ___ ___ ___ ___

TIME SIGNATURES

$\frac{2}{4}$	2 crotchet beats in a bar
$\frac{3}{4}$	3 crotchet beats in a bar
$\frac{4}{4}$	4 crotchet beats in a bar

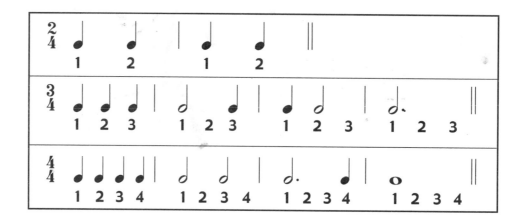

Help the space ship find the places that they may land.
Match as shown.

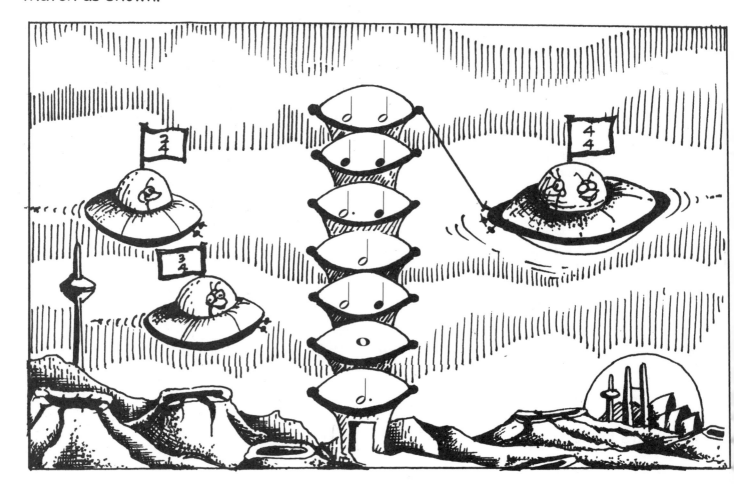

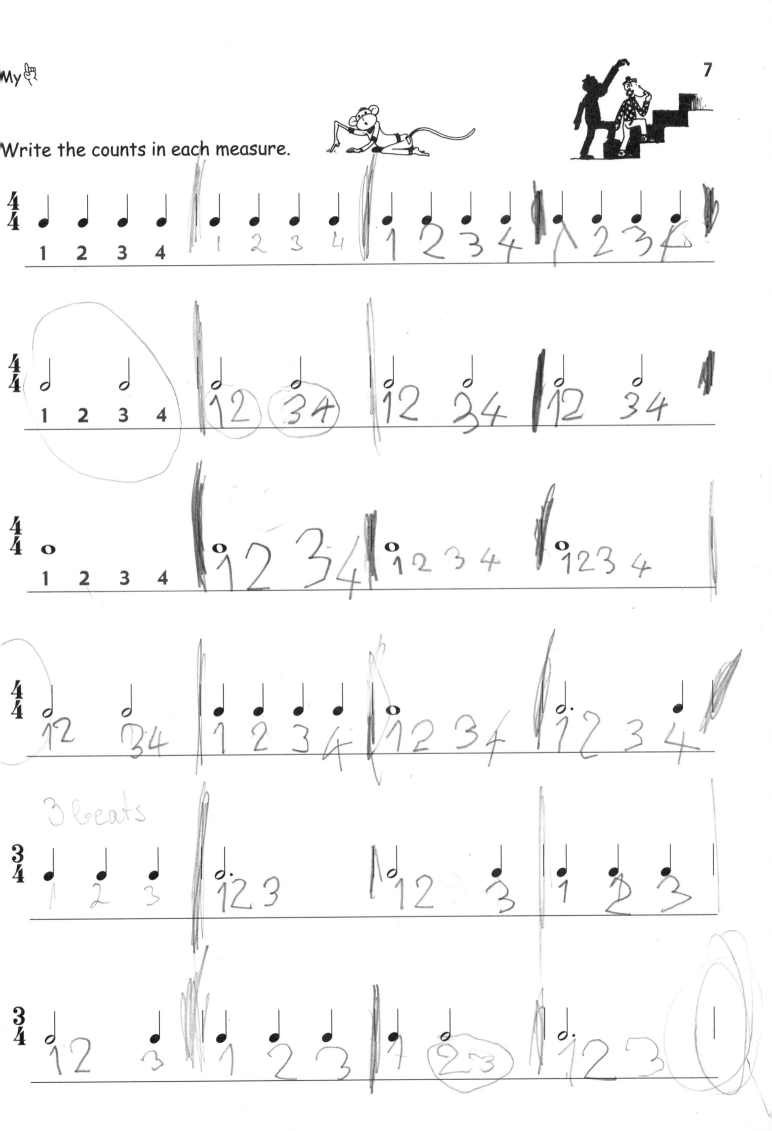

Write the counts in each measure.

 **KEYBOARD**

Print the letter-names on the white keys - C D E F G A B C D E

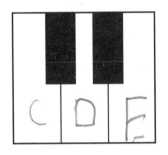

Print the letter-names on the white keys

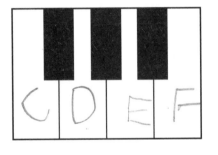

Print the letter names on the white keys

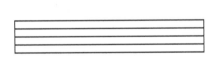

The stave consists of 5 lines

bar

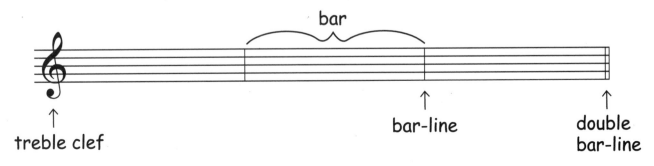

↑
treble clef

↑
bar-line

↑
double
bar-line

NOTES IN THE TREBLE

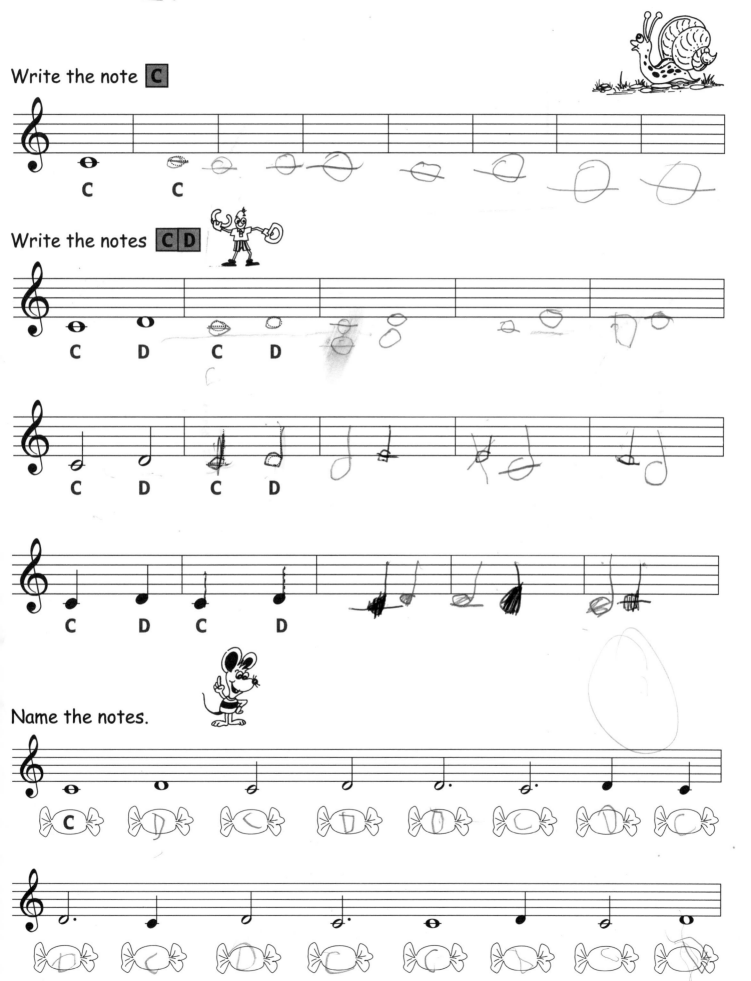

Write the note C

Write the notes C D

Name the notes.

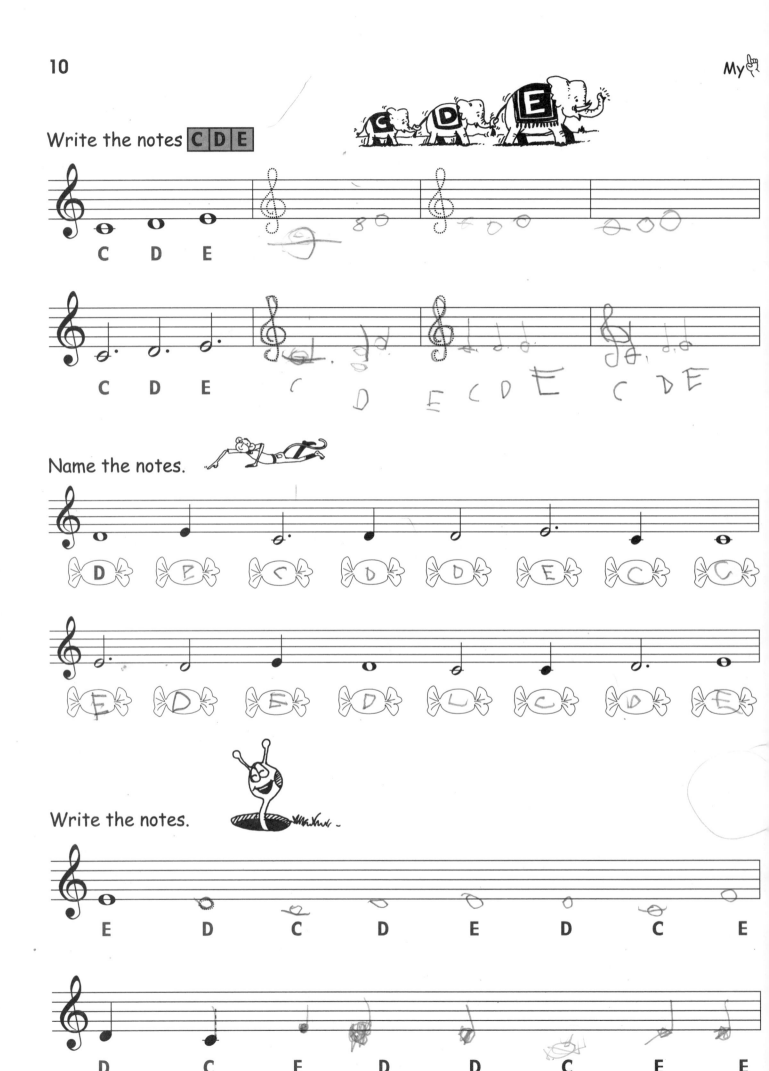

Write the notes **C D E**

C D E

C D E

Name the notes.

Write the notes.

E D C D E D C E

D C E D D C E E

Match the notes to the correct alphabets.

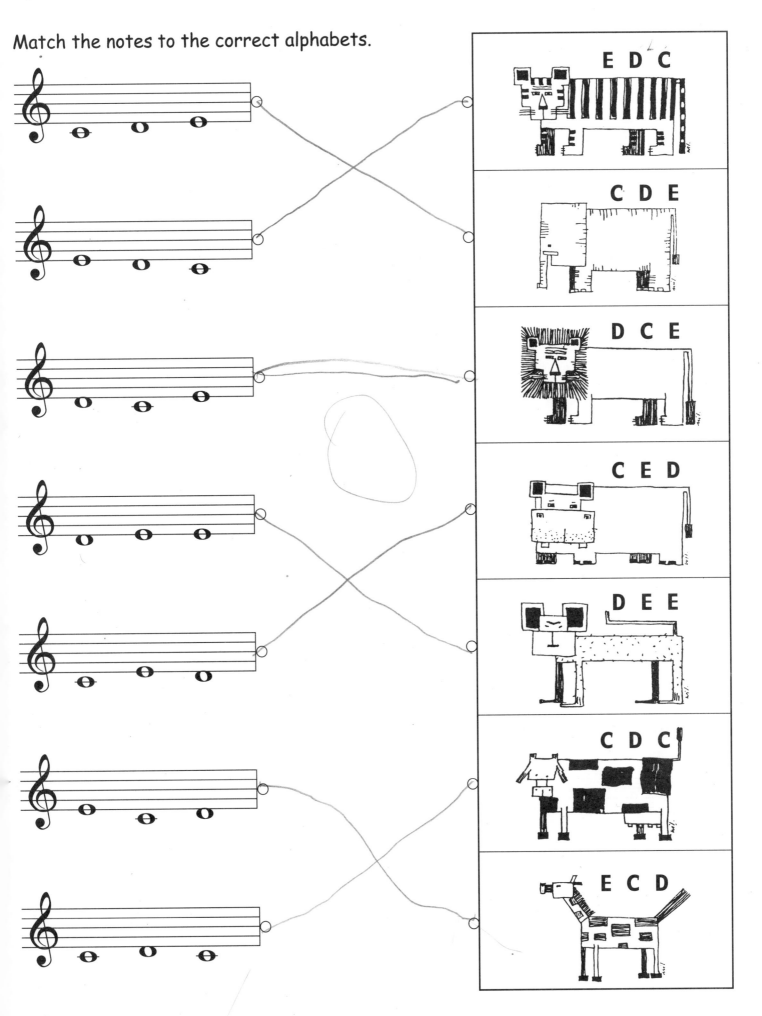

My

Write the notes **C D E F**

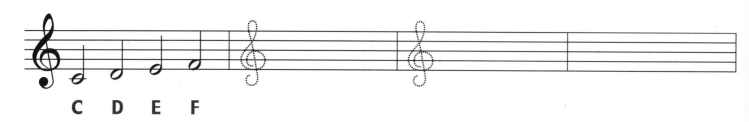

C   D   E   F

C   D   E   F

Name the notes.

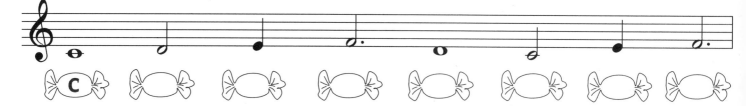

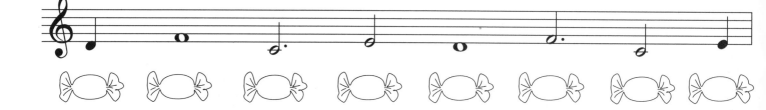

Write the notes.

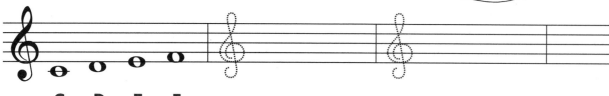

C   D   E   F   D   E   C   D

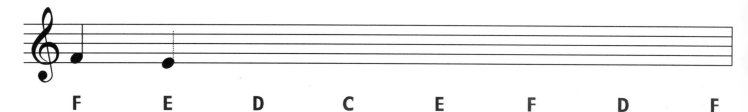

F   E   D   C   E   F   D   F

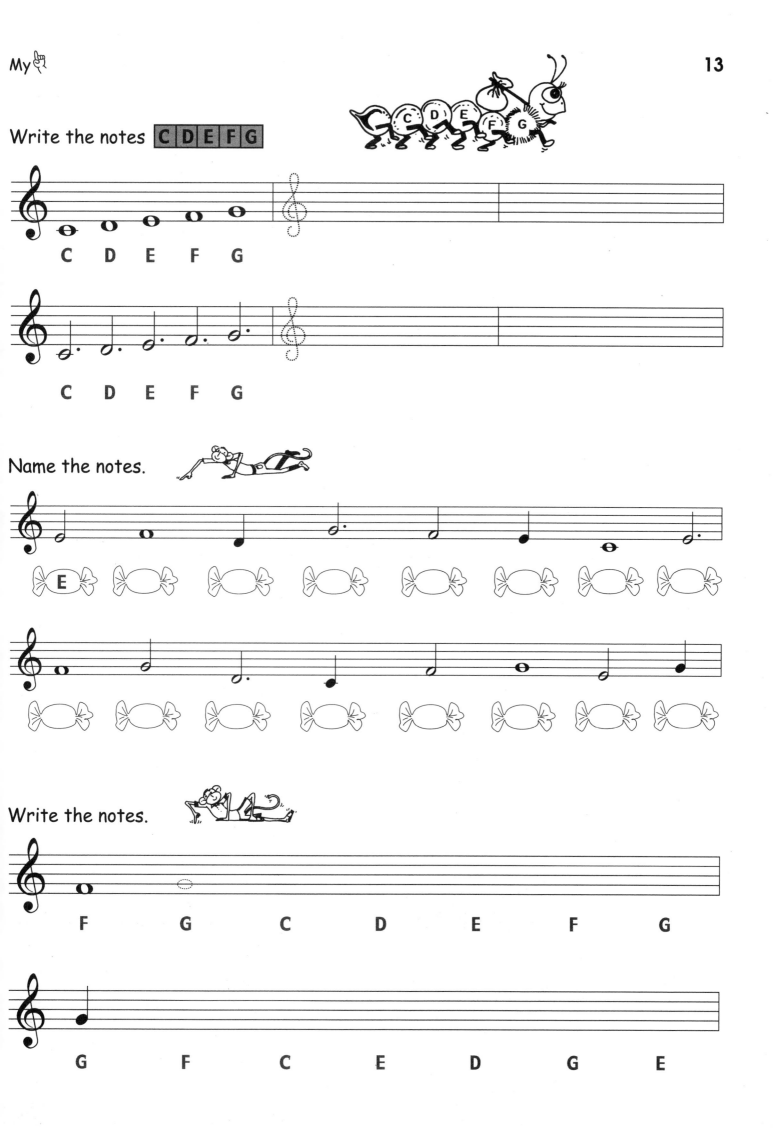

Write the notes   C D E F G

C   D   E   F   G

C   D   E   F   G

Name the notes.

E

Write the notes.

F   G   C   D   E   F   G

G   F   C   E   D   G   E

GOING CARROTS

Study the picture below and answer the questions.

Which rabbit will find the carrots?   Rabbit_____

Which rabbit will be bitten by the snake?   Rabbit_____

Which 2 rabbits will meet?   Rabbit_____ & Rabbit _____

Colour on the keyboard the notes you have to play.

1 C E G	**5** C E F
2 D F G	**6** D E G
3 C D F	**7** C D G
4 E F G	**8** D E F

NOTES IN THE BASS

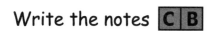

Write the notes **C** **B**

C B

C B

Name the notes.

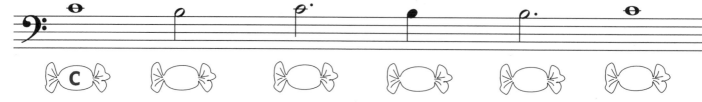

C

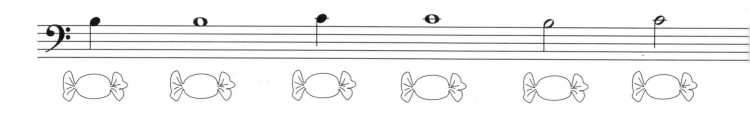

Write the notes.

C B B C B C

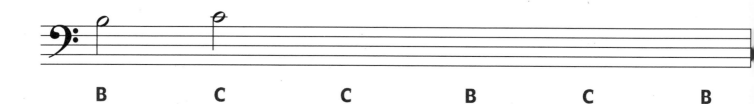

B C C B C B

Write the notes **C** **B** **A**

C   B   A

C   B   A

Name the notes.

Write the notes.

C   B   A   B   A   C

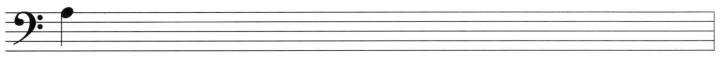

A   B   C   A   C   B

Match the boxes.

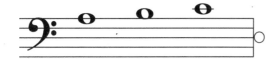

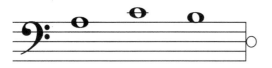

Write the notes C B A G

C B A G

C B A G

Name the notes.

A

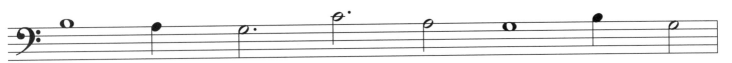

Write the notes.

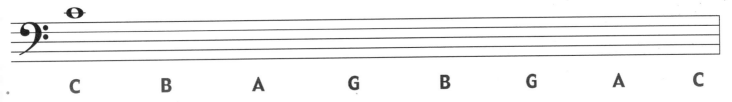

C B A G B G A C

B C G A B C G A

Write the notes **C B A G F**

C   B   A   G   F

C   B   A   G   F

Name the notes.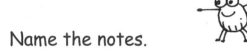

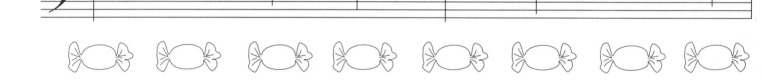

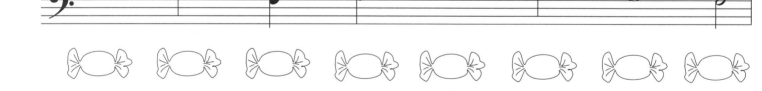

Write the notes.

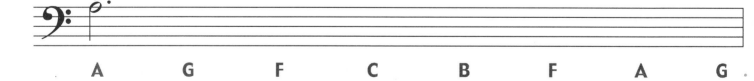

A   G   F   C   B   F   A   G

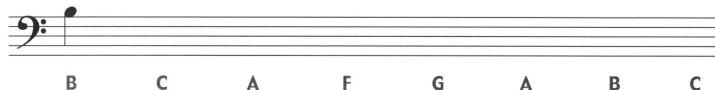

B   C   A   F   G   A   B   C

Match the notes to the alphabets.

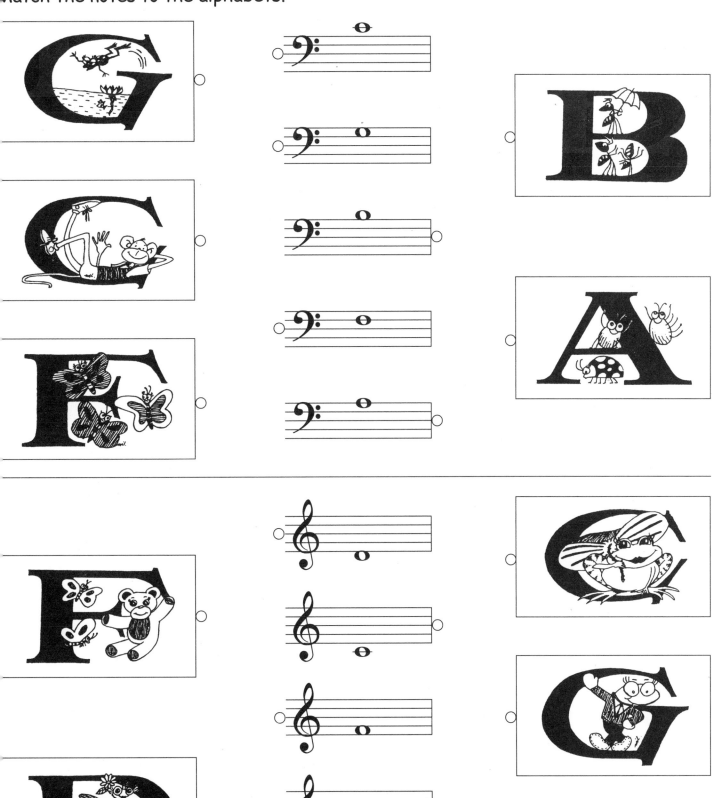

My 𝄞

Form the words and match to the pictures.

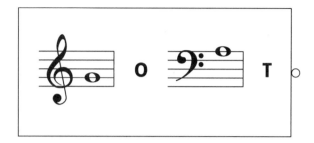   O   T

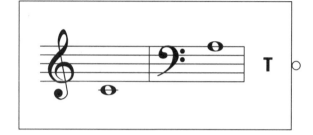   T

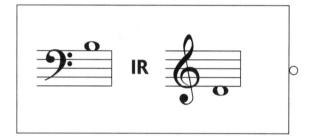   IR

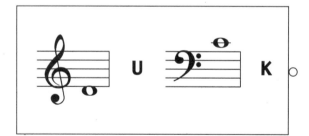   U   K

TI      R

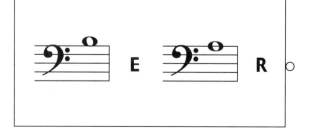   E   R

 **RESTS**

Copy the rests and number of counts.

Semibreve

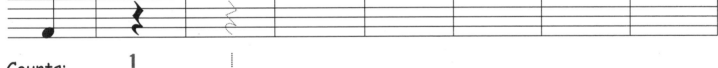

Counts: _____ **4** 4 _____

Minim

Counts: _____ **2** 2 _____

Crotchet

Counts: _____ **1** ¦ _____

Write the number of counts.

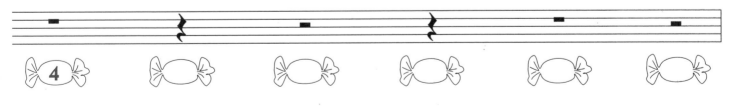

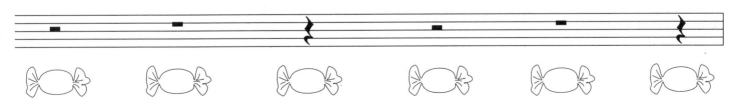

Copy the following.

1 2 3 4   1 2 3 4   1 2 3 4   1 2 3 4   1 2 3 4

Copy the following.

1 2 3 4   1 2 3 4   1 2 3 4   1 2 3 4   1 2 3 4

FIND THE PARTNERS

Help the boys find their partners.
Colour the clothing according to the time-values.
Has everyone found a partner? _____

COUNTS	COLOUR
1	RED
2	BLUE
3	YELLOW
4	GREEN

Write the counts in these measures.

1   2   3   4

My

Put in bar-lines.

Complete each bar with ▬ or 𝄽

Complete each bar with 𝅗𝅥. 𝄽

ACCIDENTALS

♯	sharp	=	raises a note 1 semitone in pitch
♭	flat	=	lowers a note 1 semitone in pitch
♮	natural	=	restores a note to its original pitch

Trace the accidentals.

Put a sharp (♯) before every note.

Put a flat (♭) before every note.

Put a natural (♮) before every note.

Name the notes.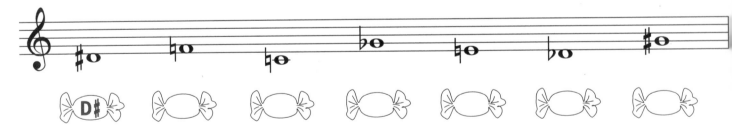

D♯

Write the notes.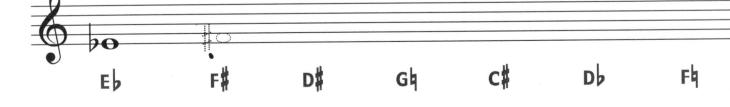

E♭   F♯   D♯   G♮   C♯   D♭   F♮

At The Baby-Sitters

1. Write the correct sign (♯, ♭, ♮) on the babies to show family connection.
2. Put your finger at ✱ and trace the route.
3. After work, Mimi, Lili and Lulu went to fetch their children.
   They fetched Mimi's baby, then Lili's and Lulu's.

What is 1) Mimi   -   _____ (cat, duck, rabbit)
          2) Lili   -   _____ (cat, duck, rabbit)
          3) Lulu   -   _____ (cat, duck, rabbit)

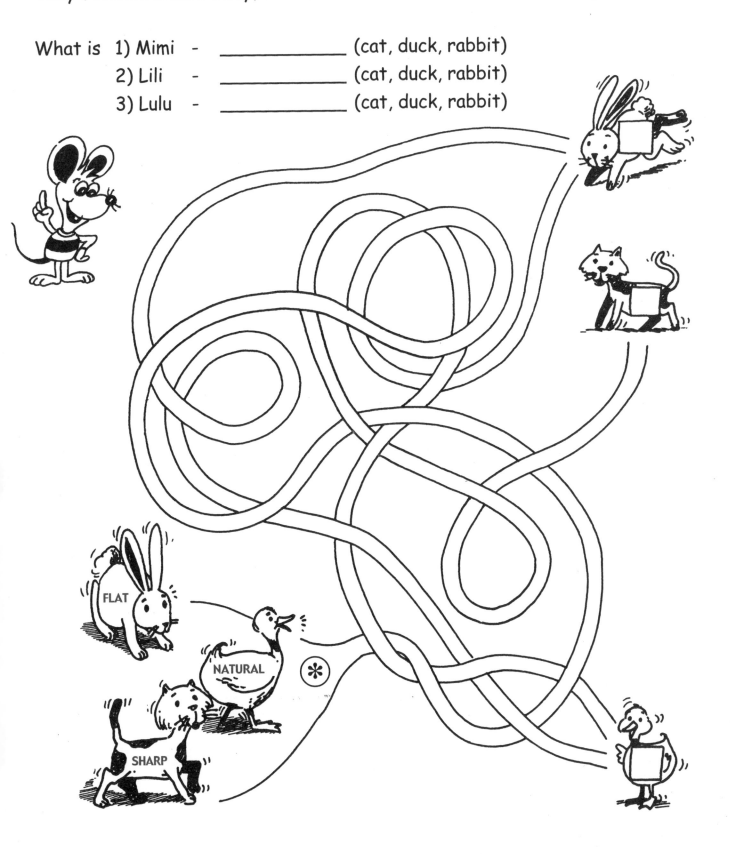

My

Name the notes.

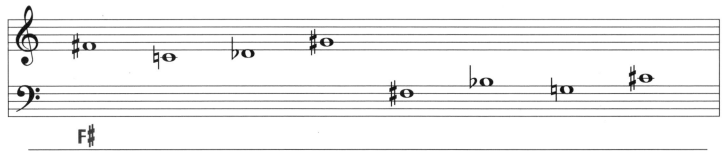

F♯

To which note does the sign belong?

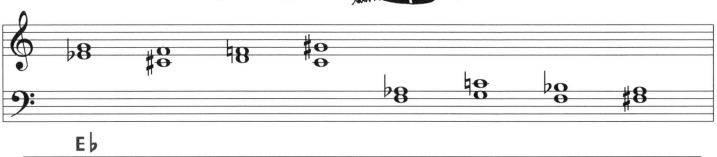

E♭

Prefix the accidental against the note stated.

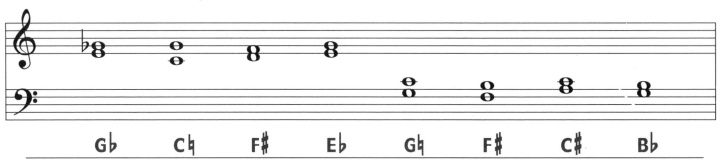

G♭   C♮   F♯   E♭   G♮   F♯   C♯   B♭

To which note does the sign belong?

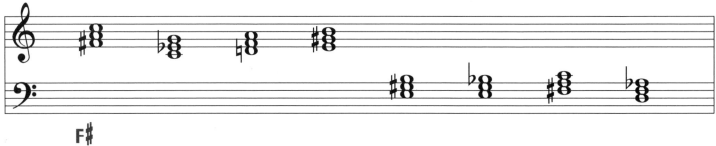

F♯

POSITION OF STEMS

The stems indicate either P or d Pond

stems up   up   or   down   stems down

Add a stem to every note.

TIME SIGNATURES

Write the counts and then the time signatures.

1 2

FISHING

These animals are fishing by the river.
Have they caught the correct fish?
Mark (✓) or (✗) on their caps.

My

COMPLETE BARS WITH NOTES

Complete each bar with

COMPLETE BARS WITH RESTS

My ☝

✳ ▭ A bar rest is used to fill an empty bar of $\frac{2}{4}$, $\frac{3}{4}$, $\frac{4}{4}$ time.

Complete each bar with 𝄽 ▬ ▬

My

TesT

TOTAL MARKS	
100	

NAME: _____   DATE: _____

20	

1. Name the notes.

2. Write the number of counts.

10	

3. Complete each bar with notes or rests.

20	

4. Write the notes.   `20`

D♯   F♯   C♮   E♭   G♮

B♭   C♯   A♮   F♯   G♭

`10`

5. Write a rest in each bar, equivalent to the value of the notes.

6. Write the counts and then the time signatures.   `2/4  3/4  4/4`   `20`